MW00694890

Especially for:

Tom

Love

From:

" _Mrs Whaley_ "

Date:

Christmas 2016

Let Every
Heart Prepare
Him Room

An Advent Devotional

Let Every
Heart Prepare
Him Room

Jean Wise

BARBOUR BOOKS
An imprint of Barbour Publishing, Inc.

Print ISBN 978-1-62836-906-9

eBook Editions:
Adobe Digital Edition (.epub) 978-1-63058-596-9
Kindle and MobiPocket Edition (.prc) 978-1-63058-597-6

All scripture quotations are taken from the King James Version of the Bible.

Published by Barbour Books, an imprint of Barbour Publishing, Inc., P.O. Box 719, Uhrichsville, Ohio 44683, www.barbourbooks.com

Our mission is to publish and distribute inspirational products offering exceptional value and biblical encouragement to the masses.

Member of the
Evangelical Christian
Publishers Association

Printed in China.

Let Every Heart
Prepare Him Room

✦

*W*ouldn't it be nice to celebrate Christmas simply, without all the hype and stress? Let this book guide you through the Advent season, preparing your heart for a deep and meaningful celebration of Jesus' birth.

Let Every Heart Prepare Him Room—An Advent Devotional will encourage you to "reduce the clutter" of the Christmas season, making room for Jesus in your life. Through twenty-eight lyrical, encouraging devotionals, you'll be reminded of God's great love, often obscured by the busyness of the season but always available to those who will consciously quiet their hearts to receive it.

In the pages to follow, you'll also find relevant quotations and prayers, plus practical tips for simplifying the holiday season. We pray that this book will change the way you view Christmas—and draw you ever closer to the baby of Bethlehem who will one day return as King of the whole world!

THE PUBLISHERS

WEEK I:
Preparation

Preparing Him a Habitation

The LORD is my strength and song, and
he is become my salvation: he is my God,
and I will prepare him an habitation;
my father's God, and I will exalt him.
EXODUS 15:2

People packed the road to Bethlehem. The masses
entered the congested streets of the village, joining
the crowds who arrived earlier for the census. Where
would Mary and Joseph find a place to stay?

With lodging scarce, Joseph worried—there
was no room in the inn. Only the shelter where the
animals lived stood empty, certainly not the type of
home they hoped and imagined as the birthplace for
their child.

Perhaps they began at once to make preparations.
Maybe Mary swept the floors and swung open the
doors for fresh air to enter. The animals watched
as Joseph removed what was unnecessary and
rearranged whatever remained in the room that
might get in the way when the child arrived. He
probably scrubbed the manger in preparation for
the Christ Child.

"He is my God, and I will prepare him an
habitation."

Habitation is a place to dwell and a location
where we return on a regular basis. In today's world
we use the word home more often in our language

than habitation. Home comes from the Old English word *ham*, referring to a gathering of people. Another definition describes home as an abiding place of affections.

Home is where love dwells.

Mary and Joseph prepared a home for the newborn Jesus. If we knew God would be stopping by our homes today, how would prepare for His visit?

In preparation for company, we sweep and pick up the unnecessary clutter lying around the house. We clean, dust, and polish making everything shine and sparkle. Maybe we decorate with something special or cook a tasty treat to create a warm welcome for our guest.

Our hearts can be prepared to welcome the Christ Child during Advent in the same ways.

Like Mary, we sweep out the dirt and darkness of sin. We let go of unnecessary emotions. We ponder what blocks us from fully welcoming God and remove unnecessary obstacles. We choose to spend less time on busy work and more time with God.

We unlock the windows of our hearts with music, prayer, and silent time with the Father of the Christ Child. The openness of our hearts allows the Holy Spirit to bring in the fresh air of the season.

From God's heart to our hearts and from God's home to our home, we prepare a habitation for Christ.

Lay not up for yourselves treasures upon earth, where moth and rust doth corrupt, and where thieves break through and steal: But lay up for yourselves treasures in heaven, where neither moth nor rust doth corrupt, and where thieves do not break through nor steal: For where your treasure is, there will your heart be also.
MATTHEW 6:19–21

*L*ORD, *thou hast heard the desire of the humble: thou wilt prepare their heart, thou wilt cause thine ear to hear.*
PSALM 10:17

I will honor Christmas in my heart,
and try to keep it all the year.
CHARLES DICKENS

*

The only real blind person at
Christmastime is he who has
not Christmas in his heart.
HELEN KELLER

Encouragement

Pay attention this week to times
you worry, complain, or become
preoccupied with unfinished business
that distresses the mind and heart.
Let it go and leave room for God
to dwell within you.

✦

Prayer

Lord, I want to honor You
by preparing my heart for You.
Create in me a pure heart and
renew a right spirit within me.

What Is in Our Hands?

And the LORD said unto him,
What is that in thine hand?
EXODUS 4:2

Trying to save time and trips, I grabbed the packages
and balanced them on top of one another. I slowly
entered the kitchen from the garage, pleased with
my efficiency. If I juggled this load correctly, I could
handle everything. I did well until I reached the
closed door and had no way to open it.

Advent sometimes feels that way. Busy schedules
with cards to write and company coming pack the
moments of our lives. The calendar fills with parties,
extra church services, and Christmas programs.

Even if our datebook is empty, our fidgety hands
may hold worry, loneliness, and anger. With hands
loaded with bags of emotional burdens, we are
unable to open the door into this season.

Hanging onto the wrong things, we can't find
a way to begin a time of quiet preparation for the
Christ Child. What are we clinging to so tightly we
can't reach out to God? How do we prepare our hearts
for Advent?

The Lord asked Moses in this verse, "What is
that in thine hand?"

Moses answered, "A rod."

Then the Lord told Moses to cast it on the ground. As Moses let it go and the rod fell to the ground, it became a serpent. Moses left it there and took off in the new direction where God led him.

We, too, need to answer the Lord's question and name the things that fill our hands. We suspend what we are doing, step back from all the preparations, and evaluate what we keep and what we set aside. Letting go of our agendas, we then can pick up what God wants us to do.

God wants to give us a full life. We can't receive this gift if our hands are full of other things. Instead, allowing the world and expectations to control our thoughts and actions, we come to him with open hands so he determines how we spend this season.

We can practice the palms down, palms up prayer. Coming to God, we physically lay our hands open with our palms downward, imagining all we cling to dropping like Moses' rod. Then with palms upward, we offer our empty hands to God for His gifts of Advent.

Just the physical act of opening our hands in prayer slows us down to find God.

This season let's cling more to what we cherish than filling our hands with empty and meaningless details. Open hands enable us to extend our hands to others and to touch God.

Open hands. Open hearts. A space for God to enter.

*If thou prepare thine heart, and stretch
out thine hands toward him; for then shalt
thou lift up they face without spot; yea,
thou shalt be steadfast, and shalt not fear.*
Job 11:13, 15

*Draw nigh to God, and he will draw nigh
to you. Cleanse your hands, ye sinners;
and purify your hearts, ye double minded.*
James 4:8

When there is no time to do it, that's when
you most need to unclutter the calendar
and go apart to pray. When the gridlock in
your schedule relentlessly forbids, it is the
time you most need retreat. That is when
your heart beats against the prison walls of
your enslavement and says, "Yes, Lord,
I want to spend time with you."

EMILY GRIFFIN

A prison cell, in which one waits,
hopes. . .and is completely dependent on
the fact that the door of freedom
has to be opened from the outside,
is not a bad picture of Advent.

DIETRICH BONHOEFFER

Encouragement

Take time this week in prayer to
practice the palms down, palms up
technique of praying. With hands
facing down, purposely let go, and
then with hands held upward,
offer your heart to God.

※

Prayer

Dearest Lord God, my hands ache
from clinging too tightly to the cares,
concerns, and contents of the world.
I ask for courage to release my grip
and to receive You with open
and willing hands.

Pushing the Mute Button

*Lord, thou hast heard the desire of the
humble: thou wilt prepare their heart,
thou wilt cause thine ear to hear.*

PSALM 10:17

✦

Commercials blare "Buy, buy, buy!" People stand on
street corners with signs telling us where to find the
best deals of the day. Stores broadcast advertisements
over their loudspeakers, hang banners from the
ceilings, and paste glossy notices to the floor
proclaiming the latest gift ideas—all intended to
invoke shoppers to purchase more stuff.

Even friends and family tell us what we need to
do. They chat about the current must-have items or
the ideal Pinterest creation to make for the perfect
decoration. We wonder if we have done enough as we
pay attention to our neighbor's outside trimmings,
the clamor of discontentment increasing in our
hearts.

Our own internal critic complains that we aren't
good enough or haven't bought enough or we need to
do more to make this season just right.

After a while, the deafening roar of the world
and the internal racket of our egos take over our
entire being. The blaring jars our spirits and pollutes
our hearts. All we hear is *buy*, *do*, and *do more*.

Our souls are desperate to hear the whispered

peace of Advent. What we listen to during Advent contributes to the preparation for this season. Where can we find this tranquility?

Preparing our hearts for Christ's coming arrival, we ask God to help us push the MUTE button. As children of God we separate ourselves from the hubbub and enter His stillness by taking a few minutes each day for quiet.

We pause for silence in the morning. We can find quiet moments at the start of a meal, as we wash the dishes or turn the blanket down for sleep.

We lower the volume on the music of the season. Humming a hymn instead of trying to remember the words quiets us and brings us peace.

We listen to the lyrics and ponder how they invite us to slow down and hear God.

We take in the precious sounds of our loved ones' voices and the delightful giggles of children.

We savor the words written on cards from friends far away.

We listen to our hearts instead of the rambling clamor of our minds. What we say to ourselves often takes away the peace. We make space in our hearts for God by creating an oasis of silence to ponder the Christ Child.

What are our hearts listening to this year? Push the MUTE button and hear the coming of the Christ Child.

*Happy are thy men, and happy are these thy
servants, which stand continually before thee,
and hear thy wisdom.*
2 CHRONICLES 9:7

*Bow down thine ear, and hear the words of the wise,
and apply thine heart unto my knowledge.*
PROVERBS 22:17

When the world quiets to the
sound of your own breathing,
we all want the same things:
comfort, love, and a peaceful heart.
MITCH ALBOM

The trees, the flowers,
the plants grow in silence.
The stars, the sun, the moon move in silence.
Silence gives us a new perspective.
MOTHER TERESA

Encouragement

Read Luke 1:18–23, 64 about
Zacharias and his time of silence.
What was that like for him
to remain quiet for so long?
Set aside an hour, half day,
or even longer for silent
listening to God.

✦

Prayer

Lord of silence and sound,
cleanse the ears of my heart to hear
Your voice this season.

Ready, Set, Rest

*Wherefore seeing we also are compassed about
with so great a cloud of witnesses,
let us lay aside every weight,
and the sin which doth so easily beset us,
and let us run with patience the race
that is set before us.*

HEBREWS 12:1

---

*R*eady. Set. Go.

We are off to the races as the holidays begin. In the latter part of the calendar year we hurry from one special event to another. We barely catch our breath or find our souls in the rush of one season piled upon another.

The frenzy begins with Labor Day and the start of school. Halloween and Thanksgiving rapidly follow. Then Christmas descends upon us.

No wonder we feel like a train wreck by the time December 25 arrives.

We organize what we need to buy. We change the decor and colors with each month. We celebrate special days, but do we enjoy and savor the time?

Advent gives us an opportunity—not for one more season to *do*, but for a season to *be*. We discover a time to take a deep breath and enjoy the journey. This period before Christmas contains precious moments for us to relish the extraordinary gift of our Savior.

Life can feel like a race, and the stress of

decorating, celebrating, and planning holidays' burdens weigh us down. Like runners, we must lay aside excessive duties and rest in the light of the Christmas story. Can you imagine long distance runners carrying a heavy backpack and dragging luggage while they run?

Advent is the refreshment stand in the marathon. Advent offers a time to cool down and renew our spirits before the New Year. We drink in His presence and linger in His light for warmth and nourishment. We quench our thirst at His well.

Hebrews encourages us to lay aside every weight and run with patience the race before us. We are like runners at the starting line.

Runners get ready. We prepare for the season knowing our destination is not perfection, but the baby in the manger.

Runners get set. We pause, pose, and focus on the finish line. We embrace moments of stillness for a minute and steady our eyes only on the Christ Child.

Instead of a mad dash, we rest. We acknowledge that our racing won't accomplish what we need, and our true aim of Advent is to create space for God.

We enjoy the moments with God. We thank Him for the gift of His Son. We express our gratitude for the light in a time of darkness. We rest in the time of rush.

Knowing a great cloud of witnesses cheers us on, we continue forward into a new year refreshed from the restful peace of Advent.

Return unto thy rest, O my soul;
for the LORD hath dealt bountifully with thee.
PSALM 116:7

For David said, The LORD God of Israel
hath given rest unto his people,
that they may dwell in Jerusalem forever.
1 CHRONICLES 23:25

Hurry ruins saints as well as artists.
THOMAS MERTON

✳

It is not enough to be busy; so are the ants.
The question is: What are we busy about?
HENRY DAVID THOREAU

Encouragement

Set a timer for twenty minutes,
three different times.
For the first twenty minutes,
unclutter a room or begin one Christmas project.
For the second period, read God's word.
For the last twenty minutes,
sit quietly and listen to God.

✳

Prayer

Holy One, thank You for offering me rest and
refreshment in Your presence. I get so sidetracked
and distracted by the busyness of this season.
Slow me down, Lord. I want to enjoy Your
presence and have time to know You better.
You are my sanctuary and place of renewal.

Advent Assignments

The voice of him that crieth in the wilderness,
Prepare ye the way of the LORD, make straight
in the desert a highway for our God.
ISAIAH 40:3

✦

𝒯he annual children's Christmas pageant blends
inspiration with wonder, sprinkled with hilarious
chaos. Four-year-olds dress in white robes with
crooked gold halos. The second graders don long
bathrobes portraying shepherds. Wise men wear
scratchy fake beards and carry gifts for the Christ
Child. Those old enough to learn lines seriously
deliver their messages on time. "No room in the inn.
Go to the stable," shouts the fifth-grade innkeeper.

Mary and Joseph walk down the church's center
aisle in the grand finale. Cherub voices sing "Silent
Night" so sweetly their voices bring tears to the
congregation. All eyes focus on the manger in the
center of the activity.

The young actors practice their assignments and
know their roles. Though glitches may happen in the
performance, once again the Christmas story is told.

John the Baptist knew his role, too. He knew he
wasn't the Messiah. His job was to prepare the way
of the Lord and his role was to make straight the
highway for our God.

In the midst of Christmas preparations,
sometimes we get our roles confused. We may think

we are to portray the perfect hostess. We present the ideal family with a textbook marriage to others. Our part is the flawless decorator. We put on our masks and say our rehearsed lines.

When in reality, this season can be tattered and broken apart by lofty expectations, too little money, family feuds, and just not enough time or energy.

We can learn from John's message. He knew what he was called to do and stuck to that straight highway. The children in the Christmas pageant focused on what they were to say and do instead of trying to play every part.

Preparing our heart for the Lord implies knowing our boundaries and acknowledging our limitations.

This year who are we in the story about Bethlehem? We stick to that task and do our best.

We also honor the capabilities of others in the play of life. Maybe some just aren't able to communicate well. Often they come with crooked halos and scratchy fake beards.

Like a children's production of the Christmas story, mistakes will be made and lines forgotten. Maybe whole scenes will fall apart.

We smile, enjoy, and concentrate on the final scene of Advent. We listen with glistening eyes for angel voices in the sounds of the season. We focus on the manger in the center of the stage of our heart.

*And let the beauty of the L*ORD *our God be upon us:*
and establish thou the work of our hands upon us;
yea, the work of our hands establish thou it.
PSALM 90:17

✳

They say unto him, Lord,
that our eyes may be opened.
MATTHEW 20:33

The place to improve the world
is first in one's own heart
and head and hands.
ROBERT M. PERSIG

*

Fear less, hope more; eat less, chew more;
whine less, breathe more; talk less, say more; love
more, and all good things will be yours.
SWEDISH PROVERB

Encouragement

Focus only on one thing at a time.
Do the one thing in front of you.

*

Prayer

Lord, you've given me gifts and talents
to use in specific ways to serve you.
Help me use my abilities to
share the good news.

Stumbling Blocks and Hurdles

And shall say, Cast ye up, cast ye up,
prepare the way, take up the stumblingblock
out of the way of my people.
ISAIAH 57:14

＊

*O*uch! I ran right into the corner of the table, tripping and falling onto my knees. I walked my usual route through the dark living room, but didn't remember we rearranged the furniture to make room for the Christmas tree.

Another stumbling block on the way to Christmas.

So, too, our perfect plans for getting ready for Christmas and for embracing Advent may fall apart.

We had every intention of waking up early to read our devotional. We knew the packages needed to be mailed by December 10 and the cards addressed by the middle of December. Then the treats for the neighbors burned in the oven and now our cousin can't come to the family dinner.

The stress of the holiday adds to our shattered expectations like hurdles before a runner. The barriers of disappointment, discouragement, and weariness loom before us. All we see before us are stumbling blocks obstructing our view of the manger.

We spend more time focused on preparation for the arrival of Santa Claus than getting ready for the coming of the Christ Child.

Preparing our hearts to receive the Savior means becoming aware that obstacles threaten our path to Christmas. Taking time before we trip and fall to identify what may block us from seeing Him in Advent can prevent problems and ease frustration.

Even more difficult is to stop and consider if we are a stumbling block for others. Do our attitudes, actions, and words impede someone else? Our behavior or lack of compassion may prohibit others from seeing God in Advent.

Sometimes acknowledging what prohibits our joy during Advent can put the situation into perspective. We worry more about what others think than to remember the true purpose of the card is to wish them a joyous celebration of Christmas. After all, there isn't a law that cards have to arrive precisely on a particular date.

Begin the removal of hurdles by forgiving others and yourself. We must embrace the reality of a busy season by allowing ourselves time to rest and creating space for God to enter our hearts.

Advent is an inward preparation for the coming of Christ. Jesus is the reason to celebrate this season. Like moving the furniture to make room for the Christmas tree, we reset plans and priorities to focus on Christ. We intentionally remove what blocks us from Him. When we realize the baby in the manger is God, all the stumbling blocks and hurdles disappear.

Whoso walketh uprightly shall be saved:
but he that is perverse in his ways shall fall at once.
PROVERBS 28:18

Wherefore let him that thinketh
he standeth take heed lest he fall.
I CORINTHIANS 10:12

Nobody trips over mountains.
It is the small pebble that causes you to stumble.
Pass all the pebbles in your path and you will
find you have crossed the mountain.
AUTHOR UNKNOWN

✳

To prepare our hearts to welcome the Lord,
who, as we say in the Creed, will come
one day to judge the living and the dead,
we must learn to recognize His presence
in the events of daily life.
Advent is then a period of intense training
that directs us decisively to the
One who has already come,
who will come, and who continuously comes.
JOHN PAUL II

Encouragement

Spend a few minutes identifying the obstacles
and hurdles that block you from spending time
with God. Write them down to remove them
from your head and put them on paper
so they can be seen and managed better.
Take one step to eliminate a stumbling block.

✳

Prayer

God of clear vision, open my eyes to see
what blocks me from You. You are my priority
this season and the center of all my desires.
The world can be a dark and scary place.
Help me find strength and peace
to know You are with me.

Christ at Home Within Us

In my Father's house are many mansions:
if it were not so, I would have told you.
I go to prepare a place for you.
JOHN 14:2

✳

Homes appear different this time of year. What fun it is to drive around the neighborhood admiring all the creative twinkling lights and imaginative decorations.

Even inside our homes, the rooms transform into an altered, almost holy atmosphere. No other time of year is this space warmed with the glow of candlelight on the mantle, sweet aromas of gingerbread cookies drifting from the kitchen and laughter of bubbling anticipation from kids of every age.

We prepare for the holiday by clearing the spaces within our houses. We move the furniture, add decorations, and hang seasonal towels in the kitchen. Maybe we set out Christmas dishes and centerpieces for the table and light the wreath on the front door.

One of the main decorations is the Christmas tree. No matter its size or the style of ornaments, this is the one decoration most commonly used. Some people assemble trees in every room; others just place a small one on a table.

The larger trees may require moving furniture to make room. We may set other usual items aside so the tree fits in for its brief visit. The whole house takes on a new perspective.

In Advent we prepare our hearts for Christ. Like rearranging our homes, we intentionally get ready for His arrival.

How can we transform our hearts so we are ready? Creating a new atmosphere within us sets out the welcome mat for His coming.

Maybe we have to move some normally scheduled activities to make space. Often we have to set aside things that normally fill our time so we have time for Him.

We remember to light candles, listen to carols, and read the Christmas story. We sit quietly, gazing at the beauty of the symbols of Advent.

Just like rearranging the living room to make room for the tree, some normal activities and traditions are harder to move like the bulky couch. We may need others to help us. We may hesitate to ask for help, but by speaking up, things are arranged quickly and time left for enjoying the season.

God has prepared a place for us not only in heaven, but in Advent, too. He gives us this special time to hear and experience Him in new ways. Creating space for God during Advent opens our hearts and provides a new viewpoint of life.

Homes are transformed by the lights of this season. Our hearts, too, can change in God's light.

That Christ may dwell in your hearts by faith;
that ye, being rooted and grounded in love.
EPHESIANS 3:17

Hereby know we that we dwell in him, and he in us,
because he hath given us of his Spirit.
I JOHN 4:13

Christ asks for a home in your soul,
where He can be at rest with you,
where He can talk easily to you,
where you and He, alone together,
can laugh and be silent and be
delighted with one another.

CARYLL HOUSELANDER

Our spiritual life depends on His
perpetual coming to us,
far more than on our going to Him.
Every time a channel is made for Him
He comes; every time our hearts are open
to Him He enters, bringing a fresh gift
of His very life, and on that life we depend.
We should think of the whole power
and splendor of God as always
pressing in upon our small souls.

EVELYN UNDERHILL

Encouragement

Eat slowly this season. Practice putting down your fork between bites. Imagine Christ at your table enjoying the meal with you and you wanting to linger longer in His presence.

✦

Prayer

Welcome home, Lord Jesus.
My heart awaits Your arrival.

WEEK 2:
Pause

Singing with Grace

*Let the word of Christ dwell in you richly in all
wisdom; teaching and admonishing one another
in psalms and hymns and spiritual songs,
singing with grace in your hearts to the Lord.*
COLOSSIANS 3:16

✦

*A*rriving late one Sunday morning, I sat in a
different pew than usual. As the first Advent hymn
began, I was surprised to notice variations to the
singing I never paid attention to in my regular seat.

The young mother to my left swayed with the
music and smiled at her four-year-old who sang with
cherubic, off-key delight.

I marveled at the three elderly ladies in front
of me singing with passion, barely looking at the
hymnal—the lyrics permanently engraved on their
hearts.

My friend, recently widowed, hummed the tune
while tears welled in her eyes.

The baritone behind me passionately sang as if
performing for a king.

Advent arrived for me that morning. The music,
filled with such grace from the hearts of those around
me, opened the door of my spirit and welcomed
Christ in. God's Spirit permeates hearts through the
power of music filled with His grace.

If we pause and listen to the familiar carols
of this season, we may be surprised to find Christ

dwelling within the notes and words. The lyrics proclaim His coming and celebrate His arrival. Singing stirs our spirit to greet the Christ Child with deepened meaning. Souls find joy and hope when listening and following the Great Conductor.

Music stimulates both sides of our brains, awakens our memory, and revives our emotions. Physically, our heart rates drop and tensions lower as the tempo of a song slows. Music transforms and relaxes us.

Music changes our moods and motivates us to wonder about creative new possibilities. Music transcends the boundaries between us. Could our lives echo the lyrics of peace on earth and goodwill toward men?

Music can be the gateway into Advent. We experience Christ's arrival by simply listening, observing, and allowing music to open the closed doors to our hearts. Singing with love in our hearts to the Lord invites Him to live within us.

Taking time during Advent to deeply listen to the music of the season slows us down to spend time with God. We hear His message with a fresh point of view when we sit apart from our busyness and observe His presence in music. Singing His words this season sprinkles grace in our homes and in our hearts.

I will be glad and rejoice in thee:
I will sing praise to thy name,
O thou most High.
PSALM 9:2

Sing and rejoice, O daughter of Zion:
for, lo, I come, and I will dwell in
the midst of thee, saith the LORD.
ZECHARIAH 2:10

Beautiful music is the art of the prophets
that can calm the agitation of the soul;
it is one of the most magnificent
and delightful presents
God has given us.
MARTIN LUTHER

✦

I truly believe that if we keep
telling the Christmas story,
singing the Christmas songs
and living the Christmas spirit,
we can bring joy and happiness
and peace to this world.
NORMAN VINCENT PEALE

Encouragement

Use the lyrics of Christmas carols as a
vocal prayer this week. Don't sing the words;
say them slowly, savoring each word.

✦

Prayer

Lord of Heaven, my soul sings
Your story and praises Your holy name.
May this small offering draw
me closer to You and bring joy
and peace to the world.

Thankfulness Cultivates Hope

And there was one Anna, a prophetess,
the daughter of Phanuel, of the tribe of Aser:
she was of a great age, and had lived with an
husband seven years from her virginity;
and she was a widow of about fourscore and four
years, which departed not from the temple, but
served God with fastings and prayers night and day.
And she coming in that instant gave thanks likewise
unto the Lord, and spake of him to all them
that looked for redemption in Jerusalem.
LUKE 2:36–38

Advent begins four weeks before Christmas. This season of anticipation and hope starts immediately after Thanksgiving. Interesting to note, being grateful precedes the arrival of God's greatest gift. By giving thanks first, gratitude creates room in our hearts for hope to take root and blossom.

In the second chapter of Luke, the female prophet Anna proclaimed the coming of the Messiah. She lived until a very old age and never left the temple. Her full-time work involved praying and fasting day and night. Serving the Lord was her sole purpose.

Never giving up, Anna waited and watched for the Messiah. During that long span of eighty-four years, she continued to pray and serve God. Through prayer God created a space where Anna abided with the Lord and where she prepared to recognize the Savior.

One day this devout and faithful woman watched Mary and Joseph as they brought the child Jesus to the temple. Anna recognized this baby as the long awaited Messiah.

Her reaction was immediate. She gave thanks to God for keeping His promise and sending the Deliverer. What a moment that must have been for Anna—a dream come true to see the Savior before she died. She was ready and her instant response was to raise her hands upward in thankfulness.

Anna then spread the word to others, sharing God's good news of hope and salvation.

Anna models Advent for us with her attitude and actions. Immersing herself with prayer, she gives thanks first, knowing hope will soon arrive.

We can also begin Advent with thanksgiving. We pray for a long awaited answer to prayer. We treasure God's promises.

Anna served with faithfulness and spent time in prayer. We, too, abide with God in our prayers, Bible reading, and by listening quietly to His love. Like Anna, God will open a space within us where He may dwell in our hearts.

Anna knew the Messiah as soon as she encountered Him. We ask God to help us see others as He sees them and to find Him in all of our circumstances.

May we be like Anna this Advent, giving thanks first that leads to everlasting hope.

Enter into his gates with thanksgiving,
and into his courts with praise:
be thankful unto him,
and bless his name.
PSALM 100:4

Thanks be unto God for his unspeakable gift.
2 CORINTHIANS 9:15

A lack of a daily tonic of gratitude
results in an anemic soul, which, in turn, contributes
to a physical sense of listlessness.
A grateful soul, on the other hand,
is vibrant and animated and so permeates
your body with zest and with an enjoyment
of a life littered with gifts.
EDWARD HAYS

Feeling gratitude and not expressing it is like
wrapping a present and not giving it.
WILLIAM ARTHUR WARD

Encouragement

Keep a written record of daily Advent blessings.
Invite a friend or family member to join you
and share with each other.

✦

Prayer

Thank You, Lord.
When I realize all I have is from You,
my heart fills with gratitude.
Thankfulness creates a holy space
for You to enter, so I once again receive
You as my Savior and King.

Advent Is Selah Time

Trust in him at all times; ye people,
pour out your heart before him:
God is a refuge for us. Selah.
PSALM 62:8

Selah.

No one knows the exact meaning of this Hebrew word that is used more than seventy times in the Psalms. One definition describes *Selah* as a pause directed by the music leader at key points in a song.

Advent is a Selah time.

Selah reminds us to slow down and pause before proceeding. We rest momentarily to reflect on this time of Advent, the season of preparation for Christ's coming.

We focus and follow the Conductor who leads the music not only of this season, but our lives.

Advent Selah means we stop briefly and contemplate Christ's coming to earth. We use the idea of *Selah* to make space for God in our day, even in this busy season. As we pay attention, we find triggers to remind us to reflect, pray, and breathe during the day.

When we hear the clock strike on the hour, we talk with God. A Christmas carol prompts a prayer of praise. A smile on the face of a family member or coworker reminds us to thank God for joy and peace.

Incorporating deep breathing throughout our

day relaxes us physically but also refreshes and renews our spirit.

We take two or three deep Selah breaths upon rising in the morning and before entering the chaos of another day. We listen for God's calming voice instead of the world's demanding rush.

We approach the never-ending to-do list full of holiday, family, and work pressures with slow deep breaths that remind us to rely on God. Even a short Selah recess to relax with God—closing our eyes, inhaling Him in—can bring us into His presence.

As we end our day, we take two or three Selah breaths, reflecting with gratitude what the day brought into our lives and where God made His presence known.

When we pause and slowly breathe in God's wonderful gift, we exhale the stress and turmoil that arises over the holidays.

In a few brief seconds, we turn our hearts to God acknowledging He holds this day, this time, and this season in His hands. He is in control even when we feel shaken and befuddled by thoughts of purchases, wrapping, and organizing family times.

"Selah," the Conductor directs. As His choir, we pause during the music of this season and consider His gift—one of great cost, wrapped in swaddling clothes, and sent as a baby into our human family as our Savior.

Selah.

In God we boast all the day long,
and praise thy name forever. Selah.
PSALM 44:8

All the earth shall worship thee,
and shall sing unto thee;
they shall sing to thy name. Selah.
PSALM 66:4

Take time to be aware that in the
very midst of our busy preparations
for the celebration of Christ's birth
in ancient Bethlehem,
Christ is reborn in the Bethlehems
of our homes and daily lives.
Take time, slow down, be still,
be awake to the Divine Mystery
that looks so common and so ordinary
yet is wondrously present.
EDWARD HAY

Blessed are the ears which hear God's whisper and
listen not to the murmurs of the world.
THOMAS À KEMPIS

Encouragement

Breathe in while counting to four,
then exhale while counting to four.
Do this for several times throughout the day,
using your breath to remind you
to pause before God.

✳

Prayer

Dear Music Conductor, thank You for giving
us Selah pauses to draw us closer to You.
Help me follow Your direction
and guidance every day of my life. Selah.

Advent Expectations

My soul, wait thou only upon God;
for my expectation is from him.
PSALM 62:5

Lofty expectations overshadow this time of year. Unrealistic hopes can create feelings of disappointment, anger, and resentment. The culture of consumerism fuels a feeding frenzy of wants, "gotta haves," and "Gee, I wish..."

Commercials push the desired toys and the top electronics. We can barely maneuver down store aisles stuffed with overflowing displays. Businesses express their expectations of a better sales report than last year.

Our own expectation of creating the perfect holiday season also intensifies. We fight an internal conflict, torn between the hype of society and our hunger for stillness and intimacy with God. We want our children and grandchildren to have warm memories of family and faith. We desire peace for our neighbors throughout the world and health for those who suffer.

The word *Advent* means "coming" or "arrival" and reminds us of the anticipation and expectation held over hundreds of years by the people of Israel for the Messiah.

We, too, look for the arrival of the Christ Child.

With anticipation we seek that divine intimacy that God planted in our hearts. We hope our honoring the birth of the Messiah nourishes our faith.

Our expectations began with a young woman's unexpected encounter with an angel that dramatically changed her dreams and plans.

Throughout Advent we listen as the story unfolds in surprising ways and not at all what we would normally imagine. A pregnant virgin. Angels visiting in dreams. Poor shepherds awakened by a heavenly choir. An obscure village birthing a King. Wise men bringing gifts.

None of the characters' expectations from the well-known Christmas story turned out how they planned.

God's expectations always surpass our expectations. His dream for us transcends any of our aspirations. God's possibilities triumph over all human impossibilities.

Instead of disappointment in what the culture brings to our hearts, let's expect to be transformed this year by a fresh encounter with the One who goes beyond any imagined hopes and dreams we have.

We anticipate seeing God in the eyes of those we help. We feel His presence when we put others before ourselves. We know His strength when we give generously and help the poor.

Instead of focusing only on the preparations for company, gift buying, and being the perfect hostess, we turn our hearts on expecting Jesus' coming and see Him in unexpected people and places.

With open hands we let go of the expectations of the world and receive the gift of divine expectations from God. Expect the unexpected this Advent.

My soul waiteth for the Lord
more than they that watch for the morning:
I say, more than they that watch for the morning.
PSALM 130:6

❋

Continue in prayer,
and watch in the same with thanksgiving.
COLOSSIANS 4:2

Far away in the sunshine are my highest
aspirations. I may not reach them,
but I can look up and see their beauty,
believe in them and try to follow
where they lead.
LOUISA MAY ALCOTT

Lord, it is nearly midnight
and I am waiting for You in the darkness
and the great silence.
THOMAS MERTON

Encouragement

Brainstorm with family members
what everyone wants to experience
this Advent and identify
common expectations.

*

Prayer

Lord of Peace, come. Open my eyes to
find You in unexpected places this Advent.

Waiting with Hope and Patience

But if we hope for that we see not,
then do we with patience wait for it.
ROMANS 8:25

⁂

Waiting is difficult. We don't like waiting in store lines. We are used to fast food and microwavable dinners. Our smart phones provide us with immediate answers to all types of questions.

Most of us battle impatience in ourselves and shake our head when we see others struggling with waiting. Hope and patience are two commodities that are rare in our society.

When faced with a time of waiting—whether this occurs outside of the holidays or in the busy season of Advent—who are our companions as we wait?

Fear often stands by our side telling us to withdraw into the safety of our comfort zones. Fear closes us down and we only see the negative and feel the tension.

Fear's partner is anxiety who fidgets with our emotions and flings our feelings from one extreme to another. Another adversary, worry, destroys our peace.

Along comes anger that fuels self-doubt and damages relationships.

Standing in the shadows ready to join us are dread and annoyance who tempt us to skip Advent this year for the instant gratification of having the holidays over.

But we have a choice this Advent. We could choose while we wait to seek the more helpful friends of hope and patience. We can focus and listen to these more positive partners.

Hope removes the blinders of fear and despair and allows us to see the big picture. We become creative, unleashing our dreams for the future. Deep within the core of hope is the belief that things can change. Possibilities exist. Hope produces light in the time of darkness.

Patience means accepting that which cannot be changed and facing it with courage, grace, and faith. Researchers found that the act of waiting increases patience, and that patience seems to help people make smarter decisions and place a higher value on what they are waiting for.

Advent is a time of expectation, a season of waiting and anticipation. In Advent we look for God and find Him in His promises completed and those yet to be fulfilled.

Advent encourages us to re-learn the lost art of waiting, an art that helps us discern what is really worth having and to treasure its value. During Advent, we can discover that it is hopeful and patient waiting that gives depth and meaning to the whole of our lives.

We can choose who we will walk with this Advent. As we wait for the Christ Child to arrive, the healthier friends of hope and patience stay with us.

Wait on the LORD: be of good courage, and he shall strengthen thine heart. Wait, I say, on the Lord.
PSALM 27:14

And now, Lord, what wait I for?
My hope is in thee.
PSALM 39:7

Are we ready to receive Him?
Before the birth of Jesus,
His parents asked for a simple
dwelling place but there was none.
If Mary and Joseph were looking
for a home for Jesus, would they
choose your heart and all it holds?
Let us pray that we shall be able
to welcome Jesus at Christmas,
not in the cold manger of a selfish
heart but in a heart full of love,
compassion, joy, and peace,
a heart warm with love
for one another.

MOTHER TERESA

✦

Teach us, O Lord, the disciplines of patience,
for to wait is often harder than to work.

PETER MARSHALL

Encouragement

Spend less than 20 percent of your time
dwelling on your fears and concerns
and more than 80 percent of your
time focused on God's blessings.
Whenever you find yourself waiting,
use that time to pray.

✦

Prayer

Merciful Lord, guide me in choosing
hope and patience as my companions.
Help me see Your gifts in times of waiting
and remind me that You are
always present with me.

Sabbath

Six days shall work be done:
but the seventh day is the sabbath of rest,
an holy convocation; ye shall do no work therein:
it is the sabbath of the LORD in all your dwellings.

LEVITICUS 23:3

Advent is Sabbath time.

Sabbath means "to rest." Mark Buchanan writes "Sabbath's golden rule: Cease from what is necessary. Embrace that which gives life."

Advent is Sabbath time.

We rest in God's presence, eagerly anticipating the arrival of the Savior.

We savor the ordinary happenings of baking cookies, enjoying the smiles of friends and neighbors, humming carols that convey memories of Christ's first coming as the baby in the manger.

Sabbath implies holding lightly our endless list of things to get done and to be open to the invitation to be with God and others. Our hearts are more willing to sit down and give the gift of a listening presence for a friend. We set aside time to read the story of Jesus' birth and to experience God's love as we embrace the spirit of the season.

Sabbath time is never wasted; after all, it is God's time. He waits for us to join Him and to celebrate the good news of His coming to earth two thousand years ago and His promise of His return.

Sabbath brings peace, rest, and release. Pausing for Sabbath blesses us with a sense that we do have enough—enough time, space, and hope to come to God, filling that deep yearning for Him.

Sabbath is more than a once-a-week day; it is an attitude we can adopt for any season, but especially for Advent. Sabbath is more than a space on the calendar; it is a disposition of the heart. We pay attention to finding God in our moments and to enjoying our Creator.

Sabbath brings many gifts to Advent. Honoring quiet times with God sets boundaries around a season of busyness and consumption. When we create a space for God within us, we find room also for friends and family. The spirit of hospitality grows beyond who we know into compassion to share what we have with those who hunger and want.

Unwrapping the gifts of Sabbath time within Advent we find rest. We savor moments of simply *being* and find freedom from relentless *doing*. We catch our breath, inhaling the Spirit of God.

We find joy and peace as our spirits are reborn with Jesus' birth.

When we choose to honor Sabbath during Advent, we evaluate what we consider necessary and let go of the excess and needless. We keep Sabbath by honoring what draws us closer to the Giver of life.

Advent is Sabbath time.

*It shall be unto you a sabbath of rest,
and ye shall afflict your souls: in the ninth day
of the month at even, from even unto even,
shall ye celebrate your sabbath.*
LEVITICUS 23:32

*And he said, My presence shall go with thee,
and I will give thee rest.*
EXODUS 33:14

All this hurrying soon will be over.
Only when we tarry do we touch the holy.

RAINER MARIA RILKE

✳

Why are we so unwilling to set aside Sabbath
time? Does it have to do with our fear of facing
ourselves or of facing "sacred moments"?
If I stay busy enough, I can probably avoid
both myself and God. But should I?
One day each of us will have to face God
and give an account of ourselves
and our gifts, including our use of time.

BONNIE THURSTON

Encouragement

Discover what draws you closer to God
and prioritize that practice this Advent.
Take a break from the busyness
and focus on what is important.

✦

Prayer

God of Rest and Sabbath,
reveal to me what draws me close
to You and renews my spirit.
I honor You by entering into Sabbath
rest throughout this season
and throughout my life.

Root of Jesse

And there shall come forth a rod out of the stem of
Jesse, and a Branch shall grow out of his roots:
And the spirit of the LORD shall rest upon him,
the spirit of wisdom and understanding,
the spirit of counsel and might, the spirit
of knowledge and of the fear of the LORD.
ISAIAH 11:1–2

✦

The Ash borer killed the tree in our front yard. We watched the damage slowly destroying its life, but this year its dead limbs conveyed the fatal prognosis. The stump was all that remained after we cut down the tree.

Final remains of a once-living tree stood like a tombstone in our front yard most of the summer until we could get the stump pulled out. By August we were amazed to see a small green branch emerging from the dried, dead-looking wood.

The roots continued to nourish life.

The Root of Jesse has long been a symbol of Advent. From the Old Testament, Ruth and Boaz had a son named Obed who had a son named Jesse. Jesse was the father of King David. God promised David that His kingdom would last forever and through David's family, the world would be saved.

The prophet Isaiah told of Jesus' coming using the symbol of the Root of Jesse. A branch is a sign of new life and new beginnings. Jesus, as a descendent of King David, is this new branch.

The Root of Jesse represents the promise from God that came true with the birth of Jesus. His genealogy emerges from the stories in the Bible, all pointing to His arrival in Bethlehem.

With roots deep into the past and branches that stretch forth into the future, God's story of redemption for the people He loves continues to grow.

Many homes during Advent decorate a branch or small tree as a Jesse Tree. The ornaments of various symbols remind us of God's promises from both the Old Testament and the New Testament.

Signs of hope, like a dove, a candle, and the manger may appear on the decorations. Scripture often adorns each ornament retelling the accounts of Noah, Moses, and Esther.

Some families make homemade ornaments to dress up a branch from their own yards. With a deeper understanding of God's promises found in Bible stories, children and the adults put their focus on the true meaning of Advent.

We thought the tree in our front yard was dead, yet deep down its roots continued to provide life. We celebrate the birth of Jesus, the shoot from the stump of Jesse, and anticipate with hope His second Advent and the completion of all of God's promises of new life.

For if the firstfruit be holy, the lump is also holy:
and if the root be holy, so are the branches.
ROMANS 11:16

※

I Jesus have sent mine angel to testify
unto you these things in the churches.
I am the root and the offspring of David,
and the bright and morning star.
REVELATION 22:16

Hope begins in the dark,
the stubborn hope that if you just
show up and try to do the right thing,
the dawn will come.
You wait and watch and work:
you don't give up.
ANNE LAMOTT

✳

If our lives are ruled by the spirit
of Advent, this loving expectation of God,
they will have a quality quite different
from that of conventional piety.
For they will be centered on an entire
and conscious dependence upon the
supernatural love which supports us;
hence all self-confidence will be
destroyed in them and replaced
by perfect confidence in God.
EVELYN UNDERHILL

Encouragement

Make a list of symbols for Jesus and His story and find ways to incorporate them into your daily life. For example: He is the Light, so have dinner with candles. . .or listen to harp music to remind you of Jesus' lineage to King David.

✦

Prayer

Root of Jesse, thank You for Your love that strengthens my roots, providing nourishment for my journey on this earthly life.

Week 3:
Ponder

Pondering

But Mary kept all these things,
and pondered them in her heart.

LUKE 2:19

✦

What does it mean when Mary pondered all of these things in her heart?

Ponder originates from the Latin word to "weigh." Weighing something usually involves holding that item still for a few moments to allow some type of calculation to occur. When we ponder, we consider quietly and deeply. We ponder when something significant has occurred or we have a decision to make. We weigh the matter in hand.

Ponder implies reflecting and dwelling on a topic as a way to estimate the worth. Mary remembered every last detail of her experience—the sights, the smells, the sounds—from the moment of the angel's first visit to the birth of the Son to the words of the shepherds. She pondered and recognized the cost. This is a moment she will never experience ever again. Mary treasured the entire event, cementing the memory with all of her senses. She grasped the wonder of what God had done in that moment.

Pondering sounds like a process that occurs in the brain, like thinking. But Mary pondered in her heart. By using both her head and her heart, she looked at all that had happened holistically and tried to comprehend this extraordinary experience.

Mary endured much during a very short period

of time—an angel visiting, an unplanned pregnancy, sharing the news with Joseph and the family. Uprooted from her home to travel to Bethlehem, Mary gave birth in an unknown, unassuming place. Strange visitors approached her, adoring her child and bringing unusual gifts. She gazed at this baby in her arm knowing she cuddled God's Son.

No wonder she needed a moment to collect her thoughts.

When we hear the Christmas story this year, we, too, can ponder the meaning of this priceless gift from God. We reflect on the promises God keeps and reveals in Bethlehem and we wait with hope for His return.

We examine the cost of this incredible act of love. We remember the gifts of love and joy. We value the intimate moment of closeness to God.

We ponder the mysteries of birth and life and know we don't fully understand. But in stillness and in prayer, we obey and keep our hearts on God's message.

Treasure the quiet moments of reflection this year. With awe and wonder, look upon the humble manger, listen to the angel's joyous message and consider the cost. Let's be like Mary this Advent and ponder Jesus.

Finally, brethren, whatsoever things are true,
whatsoever things are honest, whatsoever
things are just, whatsoever things are pure,
whatsoever things are lovely, whatsoever
things are of good report; if there be any virtue,
and if there be any praise, think on these things.
PHILIPPIANS 4:8

Ponder the path of thy feet,
and let all thy ways be established.
PROVERBS 4:26

It is the heart that experiences God,
not the reason.
BLAISE PASCAL

✦

Once upon a time, the story goes,
a preacher ran through the streets
of the city shouting, "We must put God
into our lives. We must put God into our lives."
And hearing him, the old monastic rose up
in the city plaza to say, "No sir, you are wrong.
You see, God is already in our lives.
Our task is simply to recognize that."
JOAN CHITTISTER

Encouragement

Intentionally set time aside today
to consider deeply the wonder of Jesus
being born as a baby and who
He really is in your life.

✦

Prayer

God of Wonder and Wisdom,
I cherish Your gift of joy and love.
Thank You for staying near me
as I draw near to You.

The Welcome Mat

Know ye not that ye are the temple of God,
and that the Spirit of God dwelleth in you?
1 CORINTHIANS 3:16

✳

*W*elcome mats greet people at the front doors of many of our homes. These sturdy rugs often have a friendly greeting printed on them receiving guests to the house. "COME IN." "HOWDY!" "WELCOME TO OUR HOME."

People have been welcoming guests to their homes for centuries as a form of hospitality. Ancient people would bow before strangers and prepare a feast in tribute to their presence.

In our present day, we are more leery when an unknown person knocks on our door, but we still offer warm greetings to those we know and love. Our custom is to receive them with honor and kindness. We smile and say, "You are welcomed here."

When company arrives, we don't ignore them, reject their hugs, or refuse to receive them. We don't close the blinds and lock the door. We don't send them away because we are too busy with other duties.

When company comes, we invite them in and create a comfortable atmosphere. We make them feel accepted by engaging in conversation by both talking and listening. We ask if they need anything and share what we have—food, furniture, shelter. We usually go out of our way to make sure they feel at home and at ease, wanted and appreciated.

Imagine Jesus coming to our homes this Advent. We would make sure our homes sparkled as we cleaned and decorated in preparation for His arrival. We may get out the best dishes and bake a special treat. We would probably continually peek out the curtains in eager anticipation of His appearance.

I wonder where He would sit in my house. What would He want to drink? What would we talk about?

The irony of this encounter is as we welcome Christ into the home of our hearts, we are the recipients of His gentle acceptance and abounding love. As we greet Jesus' arrival, He has already made Himself at home within us.

In Advent we put out the welcome mat for God. We remember our hearts are the temple of God and the Spirit lives within us. This season gives us the opportunity to open wide the door and invite Him inside.

In Advent we prepare our hearts and watch for His arrival. We stop in the midst of the rush and surrender our busyness as we swing open the doors of our hearts for Jesus to come home. We sit and listen to Him as a cherished friend. We relish our time together.

Jesus is coming. What does the welcome mat of our hearts say as Jesus approaches?

I was a stranger, and ye took me not in:
naked, and ye clothed me not: sick,
and in prison, and ye visited me not.
<small>MATTHEW 25:43</small>

Be not forgetful to entertain strangers:
for thereby some have entertained angels unawares.
<small>HEBREWS 13:2</small>

The soul hardly ever realizes it,
but whether he is a believer or not,
his loneliness is really a
homesickness for God.
HUBERT VAN ZELLER

All guests who arrive should be
received as Christ, for He Himself will say,
"I was a stranger and you took Me in."
SAINT BENEDICT

Encouragement

Create an atmosphere of welcome by
simmering an aromatic hot drink on the stove,
such as hot chocolate or hot cider.

✦

Prayer

King of Heaven, I open the doors
of my heart to greet You now and forever.
Your warm and accepting love fills my
emptiness better than anything else.

An Advent Journey from Fear to Faith

And the angel said unto her, Fear not, Mary:
for thou hast found favour with God.
And, behold, thou shalt conceive in thy womb,
and bring forth a son, and shalt call his name Jesus.
For with God nothing shall be impossible.
LUKE 1:30–31, 37

✴

The startling appearance of an angel upended Mary's ordinary day. Her dreams of a perfect future shattered in one single moment. An instant flashed fear within her, but later transformed her faith.

Most of us would feel frightened if an angel unexpectedly appeared. One of the angel's first words though, was "fear not."

How do we, like Mary, move from fear to faith?

The angel delivered a life-changing message to Mary. She had envisioned her life before her and this new twist led to a life of uncertainty. This was not the path she planned for or prepared for, yet she said *yes*.

An unplanned pregnancy. An embarrassing social and family incident. The overwhelming reality of who this baby was and His impact on the world. This moment changed everything.

Mary listened to every word the angel spoke to her. God would take care of the details and handle the future. After all, God loves to take what we think is unattainable, unimaginable, and hopeless and create something out of nothingness and chaos. "For with God nothing shall be impossible."

Mary lifted up the pieces of her shattered dreams in surrender to this amazing God. She let go of her hopes, her anticipated future, her precious plans—to be obedient to God.

And God reassembled the fractured parts into a stunning masterpiece.

We dream. We plan. We set detailed goals with specific dates. We imagine what our future might be and God, who is really in control, smiles and says, "Trust Me."

Mary chose to focus not on the why or the how, but on the *who*. We, too, are invited to set our eyes and heart on God.

Mary surrendered and gave her entire self to God.

Like Mary, we are called on this path to love God with all we have. To offer compassion to the person who so often let us down. Once again we attempt to build bridges in relationships, even in times of difficult stress.

Focusing on God more than our ego-driven ways strengthens our faith. Like Mary we stepped forward into a future quite different than we planned.

If we hear the angel's message, we cast aside fears of what may come. We reach out to God who waits for us to follow Him on His wild, highly improbable mission into an unknown future.

God never intended only to grant faith to a few super believers like Mary. He gives this Advent gift for all of us.

And the angel said unto them, Fear not:
for, behold, I bring you good tidings of great joy,
which shall be to all people.
LUKE 2:10

That Christ may dwell in your hearts by faith;
that ye, being rooted and grounded in love,
may be able to comprehend with
all saints what is the breadth,
and length, and depth, and height;
and to know the love of Christ,
which passeth knowledge, that ye might
be filled with all the fullness of God.
EPHESIANS 3:17–19

Give yourself fully to God.
He will use you to accomplish
great things on the condition
that you believe much more in
His love than in your own weakness.
MOTHER TERESA

✳

Fear knocked on the door
and faith answered.
No one was there.
OLD ENGLISH PROVERB

Encouragement

Journal about your spiritual journey in life:
where has your faith grown, when has God seemed
absent and when and how have you felt His love?
How have you moved from fear to faith?

✦

Prayer

Faithful Lord, You remove all fear within me
and heal me with Your love and faithfulness.
Even in times of unknown change
and shattered dreams, You strengthen
and transform me by Your grace.

Advent Treasures

For where your treasure is,
there will your heart be also.
MATTHEW 6:21

✦

*A*nnouncing: a great treasure hunt!

Advent offers us an adventure to discover the gifts often lost and ignored. To miss out on the treasures of this wonderful season is a great spiritual loss.

Advent is a unique time to explore the riches we can open this season. Listen to the stories from each week of the Advent wreath as the candles are lit. There we discover the treasures of Advent: hope, peace, joy, and love.

Hope weaves its life-giving story from the beginning of the Old Testament to the end of time. Hope is more than wishful thinking. Hope is holding with confidence the promises of God to be with us now and in the future. God's presence is the present. The optimistic expectancy became visible in the manger at Bethlehem and will break through the clouds when Jesus returns.

We unwrap the gift of peace when we linger by the manger and ponder the immense love from God. If One loves us so much He would send His only Son to us, we can find the strength to reach out to others in forgiveness and reconciliation. We look forward to the day when all countries live in peace and goodwill.

The third candle reveals joy as a treasure found in

Advent. We open our hearts to God for who He is, not what He can do for us. We take the time to enjoy our families and friends. We also set aside time to give to others just for the joy of it.

The final precious Advent treasure is the love we find this time of year. Maybe we don't hear the word spoken aloud, but if we look closely enough we see it in the faces of children, the carols we sing, and the lights bringing God's message to all. This candle's glow immerses us in God's love that we can share with one another.

The center candle is the Christ candle reminding us of the greatest gift of all: Jesus Christ, God's Son. We open this gift last in the celebration of His birth in Bethlehem. Jesus' light shines for all the world and ignites the candles of our hearts to guide others back to God. Christ stands at the center of all life, surrounded by hope, peace, joy, and love.

Advent treasures—all gifts from God. These priceless offerings from Him often get hidden in the hurry and buried in the greed of Christmas. Dig a little deeper this Advent and find God's treasures to cherish in your heart this year.

*Again, the kingdom of heaven is like unto treasure
hid in a field; the which when a man hath found,
he hideth, and for joy thereof goeth and selleth
all that he hath, and buyeth that field.*
MATTHEW 13:44

Thanks be unto God for his unspeakable gift.
2 CORINTHIANS 9:15

We can only be said to be alive
in those moments when our hearts
are conscious of our treasures.
THORNTON WILDER

Where your pleasure is,
there is your treasure;
where your treasure is,
there is your heart;
where your heart is,
there is your happiness.
SAINT AUGUSTINE

Encouragement

Make a list of simple pleasures and savor them.
Examples could be the refreshing taste
of an orange, fresh bed sheets,
the twinkling of Christmas lights,
the giggle of young children
or the laughter of friends.

✳

Prayer

Gracious Giver, help me find Your gifts of hope,
peace, joy, and love tucked into the details of this
season and lead me to share them with others.

Creating the Perfect Advent

For do I now persuade men, or God?
or do I seek to please men? for if I yet pleased men,
I should not be the servant of Christ.
GALATIANS 1:10

✦

$\mathcal{I}$ daydream about the perfect Advent.

I want everyone happy. No one upset. Smiles all around. A supportive-not-bickering family.

I imagine the perfect Christmas dinner. The table set with my heirloom china and a candlelit centerpiece. Table brimmed with the family's favorite foods. Perfect manners from even the toddlers.

The house would be decorated like a magazine. Evergreen scents fill each room. Candles flicker to create the perfect environment. The fireplace crackles and warmly toasts the room. We would have just the right amount of winter weather to put us in the holiday mood, but not ruin travel plans.

I envision presents under the tree wrapped with a Martha Stewart flair. Crisp red bows decorate the staircase and a wreath hangs straight on every door.

My hearts also yearns for my family to worship together and to focus on the birth of Christ. I pray their lives would embrace God's love for them and they obey His call.

But Advent isn't about me. This season isn't to feed my ego by impressing others or keeping up appearances. Advent isn't the time to put our energy into maintaining the mask of public image of a family without flaws. Neither is Advent for pushing ourselves into stress-filled fatigue by trying to please everyone.

Advent is for God.

God created the perfect Advent two thousand years ago. He chose the ideal family, complete with an unwed pregnant teenager and her fiancé. They journeyed on their unplanned trip to Bethlehem where there were no available rooms.

God's flawless plan included giving birth in a stable with smelly animals. Strange unexpected visitors arrived from the fields and on camels from far away. Music rang out from a heavenly chorus.

This scene would not meet our expectations for the ideal way to bring God's Son into the world. But God's standards are different from ours. He knows what He was doing then, now, and in the future.

"Perfect" means having all the desired elements present to accomplish something as complete as possible. God brought together everything needed in Bethlehem. He continues today to shape our time and experiences to His ideal.

In reality each Advent isn't picture perfect with all the details carefully planned and executed to our wishes. When we remember that Advent isn't about us, we find peace in knowing God is still in charge. God knows how to plan a perfect Advent.

A man's heart deviseth his way:
*but the L*ORD *directeth his steps.*
PROVERBS 16:9

✳

It is God that girdeth me with strength,
and maketh my way perfect.
PSALM 18:32

Too many people miss the silver lining
because they're expecting gold.
MAURICE SETTEE

✳

Let gratitude be the pillow upon which
you kneel to say your nightly prayer.
MAYA ANGELOU

Encouragement

Consider what would be your ideal Advent
and what is realistic and practical to do this season.

✳

Prayer

Holy One, may my heart seek You first.
May my mind love You more.
May my hands serve You and Yours.

It All Comes Down to Love

Jesus said unto him, Thou shalt love the Lord thy
God with all thy heart, and with all thy soul,
and with all thy mind.
MATTHEW 22:37

Advent beckons us to contemplate the astonishing wonder of God, coming to earth as a baby and as our Savior.

Advent anticipates Jesus' return, too, in His coming back for us. We don't know when, yet we are reminded to be watchful and ready.

God guides our eyes and hearts to see the manger and to comprehend the depth of His compassion. God gives us hope to light our way to pull us back into His love.

But Advent isn't about us. God wants us to think about love this time of year—His love. We are called to love God more than the traditions we celebrate each year and the plans we make.

We learn once again not to focus on greed, self, and envy, but to see God first. God gave us Advent because it is about Him, not us.

Advent reminds us how God sent His Son to earth to restore our relationship with Him. A loving God giving His all for our sake and by loving us, our love for God flows into loving others.

It all comes down to love.

We find Him loving us in the music that draws us into His Spirit.

We see God's love in the simplicity of a humble manger.

We discover God in the messages on cards and caring conversations between friends.

We experience God's comforting presence in the tears of loneliness and loss.

Surrounded by Advent's sensory refreshment, we are continuously directed back to God's love. Through the lens of God's faithfulness, joy, love and peace we see our family and friends. But we see God first.

It all comes down to love.

God gave everything in order for us to return to Him and to love Him with everything—our hearts, souls, and minds.

John 3:16 states, "For God so loved the world, that he gave his only begotten Son." God offered His Son in order to bring us back to Him. This is the true meaning of Advent.

It all comes down to love.

The manger displays Gods love for us and tells us about God's extravagant nature. His unconditional love came down at Christmas to draw us back into His waiting arms. Love removes us from the clutches of the world's temptations and pulls us closer to Him.

At Advent we celebrate Jesus' coming and anticipate His glorious return. We also come closer to God and return to Him. The motivation is love—a loving God loving us and our love for God flowing back to Him and flowing outward into others.

It all comes down to love.

A new commandment I give unto you,
That ye love one another; as I have loved you,
that ye also love one another.
JOHN 13:34

✳

As the Father hath loved me, so have I loved you:
continue ye in my love.
JOHN 15:9

Maybe that's what it all comes down to.
Love, not as a surge of passion,
but as a choice to commit to something, someone,
no matter what obstacles
or temptations stand in the way.
And maybe making that choice,
again and again, day in and day out,
year after year, says more about
love than never having
a choice to make at all.

EMILY GRIFFIN

The secret of the mystery is:
God is always greater.
No matter how great we think Him to be,
His love is always greater.

BRENNAN MANNING

Encouragement

This Advent, try to do one small act of
kindness each day: Buy the coffee for the person
behind you in line, offer a smile to the store clerk,
or take the time to visit a lonely shut-in.

✳

Prayer

Compassionate King, I come to You,
acknowledging everything I hold dear
first came from Your loving heart.
Your love for me enables me
to breath, live, and love.
You are the source of all
encompassing compassion.

None like Jesus

Know therefore this day, and consider it in thine heart, that the LORD he is God in heaven above, and upon the earth beneath: there is none else.

DEUTERONOMY 4:39

The centerpiece of Advent is not the candles or the wreath. The focal point is not the songs or the opening of the windows of the advent calendar. The whole point of Advent is to prepare our hearts and turn our attention to Jesus' coming.

Secular greediness and chaotic calendars overshadow Christmas. Too often we forget the purpose of why we observe this season. When distracted by the world's lights and distorted attractions, we take our eyes off God.

Early church fathers began the practice of Advent with fasting before Epiphany, the day many Christians were baptized. In the sixth century customs started to connect this church season with Christ coming back to earth. In the Middle Ages, Christians first associate Advent with Christ's birth. The primary intention has always been preparation for Jesus' coming.

Advent invites us to take the time to consider who God is in our lives. We remember God's presence when we were younger. We ask Him to be with us now. And we cling to His promise of staying with us and returning once again in the future.

Advent focuses on Christ in this three-fold manner of the past, present, and future.

The nativity scene reminds us of His first coming two thousand years ago. We know there is none like Him in the past.

The Advent candles tell the story of Christ's gifts of peace, hope, joy, and love present today. We hear His words of comfort and promise in the scriptures. We worship in songs and prayers and give thanks for His continual help. We know there is none like Him now.

With a deep longing and a joyous hope, we anticipate Jesus' second coming when all eyes will be fixed on Jesus—the reason why we celebrate Advent. We know there is and will be none like Him.

Advent is the season to consider in our hearts all that God has given us and done for us in our past, while we wait in the uncertainties of our present and we look forward with hope. Advent becomes a time to reflect, savor, and trust in God's promises to be with us.

Advent transforms our hearts so we realize God's presence throughout all of our lives. We see His touch in the wonder of everyday chores. We rely on His strength to face the future.

Come, Lord Jesus. Enter our past, present, and future. We can't wait for Your arrival and we know there is none like You ever in time.

For God so loved the world,
that he gave his only begotten Son,
that whosoever believeth in him should
not perish, but have everlasting life.
JOHN 3:16

Blessed be the LORD *God of Israel*
from everlasting to everlasting:
and let all the people say, Amen.
Praise ye the LORD.
PSALM 106:48

Faith never knows where it is being led,
but it loves and knows the One who is leading.
OSWALD CHAMBERS

＊

A grateful heart is one that finds the
countless blessings of God in the
seemingly mundane everyday life.
ANONYMOUS

Encouragement

Write a love letter to God thanking
Him for all He has done in your past,
how He is with you now, and your
hopes and dreams for tomorrow.

✦

Prayer

Savior, I love to sit at Your feet with
eyes only on You. There is none like
You. You are the first and last. You
hold my past, stay with me now, and
guide me into the future.

Week 4:
Promise

Stop, Drop, and Be

Behold, a virgin shall be with child, and shall bring forth a son, and they shall call his name Emmanuel, which being interpreted is, God with us.
MATTHEW 1:23

I was seven years old and helping my dad rake the fall leaves. I pushed the foliage towards him and he swept them into the bonfire.

I twirled and played in the small piles. I got closer to the fire with each spin. A spark touched the edge of my coat. For a second I just watched the flame grow, not fully realizing the danger. When the heat burnt my skin, I panicked and started to run. My dad grabbed me and, pushing me down onto the cool grass, he rolled me back and forth until the fire went out. My dad's quick action saved me.

I never forgot that scary day catching fire and my dad protecting me. My instinct to run was second nature in a threatening emergency, but only served to fuel the blaze. My dad knew the simple safety technique of stop, drop, and roll.

The first step is to stop. Movement fans the flames and hampers those attempting to put the fire out.

The second step is to drop to the ground, covering the face with the hands to avoid facial injury.

And finally, the person rolls on the ground in an effort to extinguish the fire.

Advent also has its own saving technique for

handling the stress and the heat of a busy season.

Stop, drop, and be.

Stop all you are doing and pause. The hurry and bustle of endless things to do fuels the flames of fatigue, anxiety, and restlessness. Planning for a much-needed break to praise and be with God throughout Advent creates space for Him to touch our hearts and remind us what is really important.

Drop what is unnecessary. We often lose sight of what is realistic to accomplish in the holidays. Advent is about Jesus' coming into our world. Preparing our hearts for His arrival is our priority.

Be. God wants us to be with Him all the time, even in Advent. We practice being fully present to His presence in the moments of the day. We remember that "A virgin shall bring forth a Son and they shall call His name Emmanuel—God is with us."

Stop running. God is with us. Let's be with Him.

Drop all the disorder that fills our hearts and minds. Come empty before Him, ready to receive the gift of Emmanuel, God is with us.

Be with God, the Emmanuel, who is here right now, waiting for us.

Stop, drop, and be—good advice to practice during Advent and every day.

For the truth's sake, which dwelleth in us,
and shall be with us for ever.
2 JOHN 1:2

He shall call upon me, and I will answer him:
I will be with him in trouble;
I will deliver him, and honour him.
PSALM 91:15

If we could condense all the truths
of Christmas into only three words,
these would be the words: "God with us."
We tend to focus our attention
at Christmas on the infancy of Christ.
The greater truth of the holiday is His deity.
More astonishing than a baby in the manger
is the truth that this promised baby
is the omnipotent Creator
of the heavens and the earth!

JOHN F. MACARTHUR, JR.

My, how busy we become when
we lose sight of how God loves us.

JULIAN OF NORWICH

Encouragement

Ask yourself and your family the question:
Why do we celebrate this season?
Choose an activity that symbolizes
that reason for everyone.

※

Prayer

Emmanuel, I stand in awe
of Your amazing presence.
You, God of the Universe, chose to
become human, born as a baby,
to save the world and me.
You came to be "God with us."

Names

For unto us a child is born, unto us a son is given:
and the government shall be upon his shoulder:
and his name shall be called Wonderful,
Counselor, The mighty God,
The everlasting Father,
The Prince of Peace.
ISAIAH 9:6

*C*onveying Christmas messages has existed for centuries. The tradition of mailing cards began in the 1800s in London. Previously people exchanged handwritten holiday greetings in person before the postal service took over.

Now an estimated 1.9 billion Christmas cards are sent every year. More than one billion names signed to the bottom of cards. We type newsy family letters or share handwritten updates. Maybe we insert a photo of new babies and pass on stories about special events.

In many homes as the cards are being addressed and thoughtful notes written, prayers for the recipients are also sent up. Other people start the New Year with the tradition of revisiting each card they received and pray for the people who sent them. Our message and blessing for the season connects us with friends and family.

Names. Signatures. Identification. These are the

ways to know someone. Seeing a name brings back memories. We shared something in the past with that person and long to stay connected. Knowing another name draws us closer and creates a deep attachment through our emotions.

Jesus is known by many names. When we understand His names and their meanings, we feel united with Him. His names give us a glimpse into the nature of God. This intimate knowledge about who Jesus is binds us forever in His love.

The great promise from God to send us this Savior of many names is like a handwritten greeting from God. Each of Jesus' names holds the gifts of hope, joy, and love. The message reminds us that Jesus is our Wonderful Counselor, the Mighty God, the Everlasting Father, and the Prince of Peace.

These names of Jesus reveal an aspect of God. God tells us to seek His wisdom and strength. He will direct our ways. He reminds us He will never abandon us nor forget us. He waits for us eternally. He desires to bring peace to our hearts and the world around us.

Advent is our Christmas card from God. He signs His name in the glow of the manger and the light of the cross. He seals each envelope with unconditional love to remind us He is our God.

He sends each one of us this personalized message emphasizing the many names of our savior. Written and stamped forever with His love.

God's Christmas greeting from His heart to ours.

O LORD, our LORD, how excellent
is thy name in all the earth!
who hast set thy glory above the heavens.
PSALM 8:1

And she shall bring forth a son,
and thou shalt call his name JESUS:
for he shall save his people from their sins.
MATTHEW 1:21

Hope is the thing with feathers,
that perches in the soul, and sings the tune without
the words, and never stops at all.
EMILY DICKINSON

*

Hope has two beautiful daughters:
anger and courage: anger at the way things are, and
courage to change them.
SAINT AUGUSTINE

Encouragement

What will you do with the Christmas cards
you receive this year? Recycle? Reuse?
Pray for those who sent them?

✳

Prayer

Lord, You are Wonderful, Counselor,
Mighty God, Everlasting Father, Prince of Peace.
I say these over and over again as I know they
just begin to describe the magnitude
of Your mercy and grace.

God's Time

But when the fullness of the time was come,
God sent forth his Son, made of a woman,
made under the law.

GALATIANS 4:4

Watches, calendars, clocks on smart phones—all ways we keep track and try to control time. I heard a man once say he no longer wears a watch. There are so many ways to find the time, he just has to look around.

If only we were in control of time, we could expand it longer when we wanted more time and contract it when time lay heavy on our hearts.

Some days could have thirty hours—a little more time to get all the things we think are necessary to be done before the guests arrive. We could postpone things we don't want to face if we could manipulate the clock to our favor.

Maybe we want the days to speed up so the time until loved ones arrive comes quicker. We complain and grumble when we wait at traffic lights or in a crowded waiting room. Shortening the time would ease that stay.

What if we could make time stand still—to savor precious moments, to hold the stillness of a beautiful fleeting moment, the magic of candlelight, or to remain a little longer with someone we love.

When we admit God has time in His control we

bargain with Him as if we knew the best time to solve a problem or make something happen. We demand time bend to our convenience and perceived needs.

If only we controlled time we could create the perfect ending to our story. But the reality is we don't control time, God does.

God knows "when the fullness of time" has arrived. He sent His Son at the perfect time for the world and for us.

The waiting in Advent helps us learn to trust God more and focus less on the details of when something will occur. We can accept God's promise that His timing is best, knowing the fullness of time will be the perfect moment. The assurance that God sees the entire picture gives us hope and patience.

God directs the mystical tempo of the universe in proper cadence while holding onto each beat of our heart. He maintains the seasons and guides each sunrise and sunset. As He sees to such details of the world, we know we can trust His timing in our lives.

Time management is best left to the One who invented time, He has shown us in the past His wisdom and will provide for our every need in His fullness of time.

But as for me, my prayer is unto thee,
O Lord, in an acceptable time:
O God, in the multitude of thy mercy hear me,
in the truth of thy salvation.
PSALM 69:13

He hath made every thing beautiful in his time:
also he hath set the world in their heart,
so that no man can find out the work that God
maketh from the beginning to the end.
ECCLESIASTES 3:11

Time is too slow for those who wait,
too swift for those who fear, too long for those
who grieve, too short for those who rejoice,
but for those who love, time is eternity.
HENRY VAN DYKE

Never be afraid to trust an
unknown future to a known God.
CORRIE TEN BOOM

Encouragement

Make homemade yeast bread.
While you wait for the dough to rise,
remember those who waited for
the Messiah to come and pray for
those who wait today for His return.

✦

Prayer

Faithful Lord, I put my trust in Your
wisdom and know You will take care of
all my needs in proper order and time.

Pieces to Peace

*For unto you is born this day in the city of David a
Saviour, which is Christ the Lord. And this shall be
a sign unto you; Ye shall find the babe wrapped
in swaddling clothes, lying in a manger.
And suddenly there was with the angel
a multitude of the heavenly host praising God,
and saying, Glory to God in the highest,
and on earth peace, good will toward men.*

LUKE 2:11–14

The world is broken. Family relationships shattered.
Finances ruined. Things are not working out as we
hoped and dreamed.

War breaks out. Famine steals the life from little
children. Natural disasters dominate the news as
villages disappear under walls of water or are buried
under rubble.

We shake our heads in disbelief at the perfect
Christmas settings of peace on earth and goodwill to
men. We wonder where God is in disasters that occur
far away and in our own families.

Our advent may not be a time of joy and peace
and goodwill to others. Instead of joy and beauty in
the holiness of this season, we may find we are in
dark places of brokenness, loneliness, and bitterness.

The shepherds didn't expect that evening to be
any different than previous dark nights. They listened

to the rhythm of the rustle of sheep sounds. They performed their ordinary, mundane work. Their minds squirmed with many of the same worries about families and work that we struggle with today.

But God has other plans. God loves to surprise us. God is a specialist at creating moments of divine wonder. He wakes us up with His amazing impossibilities.

God sent His angels to shake up the shepherds and bring peace to the world. God kept His agreement to send the Messiah. He is the God of kept promises and surprises.

God heals the shattered pieces of our hopes and dreams. He fashions peace from the ruins of our battles. He repairs our individual fractures, thus healing the entire world.

God sent His Son who arrived as a baby in a far away village to ordinary parents. Jesus arrived as a baby, not born in a place holy and honorable, but in a smelly stable. Then instead of sending His royal announcement to dignitaries and celebrities, He told simple working-class shepherds.

God sends the same message to us today. He is with us in our every moment. God comes to be and to stay with us wherever we are located, even in the muck and dirt of our ordinary lives.

He is God and God keeps His promises. How He does it may surprise us, but we can trust in His promise to do it. After all, He is the expert in moving pieces to peace and holes to wholeness.

And the very God of peace sanctify you wholly;
and I pray God your whole spirit and soul
and body be preserved blameless unto
the coming of our Lord Jesus Christ.
1 THESSALONIANS 5:23

And the peace of God, which passeth all
understanding, shall keep your hearts
and minds through Christ Jesus.
PHILIPPIANS 4:7

Each of us needs half an hour of prayer
each day, except when we are busy. . .
then we need an hour.

FRANCES DE SALES

※

God walks with us.
He scoops us up in His arms
or simply sits with us in silent strength
until we cannot avoid the awesome
recognition that yes, even now, He is here.

GLORIA GAITHER

Encouragement

The holidays can become
an emotional roller coaster.
Accept the times you feel anger or
sadness and know it is okay to grieve.
Value the times of laughter,
hope, and goodwill among people.

✦

Prayer

Lord of Peace, still my fearful heart
with Your divine presence.
Your calming touch soothes my
frazzled nerves and leads me beside
still waters for rest and refreshment.

The Spirit of Advent

And the spirit of the Lord shall rest upon him,
the spirit of wisdom and understanding,
the spirit of counsel and might, the spirit
of knowledge and of the fear of the Lord.
ISAIAH 11:2

What if?

What if we stopped all the fussing and frantic doing and knelt before God and said, "I'm ready"?

What if we paused for longer than five minutes and opened our hearts to welcome the Bethlehem baby?

What if we asked for God's Spirit to rest upon us and help us see His gifts in this season of Advent?

What if we made room for Jesus in our hearts?

God wants to be with us and waits for us to join Him. In our time with Him, His Spirit nurtures godly qualities within us. God's Spirit feeds and cultivates our spirit. He heals our hurts and holds us when we cry.

Isaiah shows us the answer to our "What if?" question. He reveals the gifts that await us.

Isaiah reminds us that by dwelling in God's Spirit, our vision clears and we see through His eyes of wisdom and understanding. Like Mary, we ponder in our hearts God's immense love and favor. We know we can have confidence that His plans will prevail and will work out in His time.

We find wisdom in reading God's Word, guidance from time spent in prayer, and strength from the Holy Spirit.

Pausing and resting in God's Spirit leads us forward with His counsel and might. Like Joseph, we follow God's direction in life even though the path is different from what we expected and sends us into unknown territory. With God by our side, we take one step at a time each day.

Making room for Jesus in our hearts nourishes growth of His knowledge within us. Like the shepherds, we drop everything else and race to find the unexpected baby in the manger. The presence of the newborn King ignites our passion to learn more about this God who loves us so much to send His Son to save us.

When we bow down in worship of our newborn Savior. Like the wise men we bring our gifts to lay before Him in adoration and praise. We learn not to fear God as a judge and One who condemns, but as One worthy of our honor and obedience.

His Spirit bathes us with the renewing waters of wisdom and understanding, of counsel and might, and of knowledge, awe, and wonder. The Spirit of God waits for us this Advent.

What if we joined Him?

A new heart also will I give you,
and a new spirit will I put within you:
and I will take away the stony heart out of
your flesh, and I will give you an heart of flesh.
EZEKIEL 36:26

✳

That the God of our Lord Jesus Christ,
the Father of glory, may give unto you
the spirit of wisdom and revelation
in the knowledge of him.
EPHESIANS 1:17

Lord Jesus, Master of both the light and the
darkness, send Your Holy Spirit upon our
preparations for Christmas. We are Your people,
walking in darkness, yet seeking the light.
To you we say, "Come, Lord Jesus!"
HENRI NOUWEN

It might be easy to run away to a monastery,
away from the commercialization, the hectic
hustle, the demanding family responsibilities
of Christmastime. Then we would have a holy
Christmas. But we would forget the lesson of the
Incarnation, of the enfleshing of God—the lesson
that we who are followers of Jesus do not run
from the secular; rather we try to transform it.
It is our mission to make holy the secular
aspects of Christmas just as the early Christians
baptized the Christmas tree. And we do this by
being holy people—kind, patient, generous,
loving, laughing people—no matter how
maddening is the Christmas rush.
ANDREW GREELEY

Encouragement

How will you know when you are ready
for the Christ Child? How has your heart
been transformed this Advent?

✳

Prayer

Everlasting God, You take my what if's
and lead me to solid answers
found only in You.

Every Moment Is a Gift

Every good gift and every perfect gift is from above,
and cometh down from the Father of lights,
with whom is no variableness,
neither shadow of turning.

JAMES 1:17

Gifts often become the center of attention for us this time of year. Christmas consumption monopolizes stores, screens, and souls. We let stuffed calendars and the greed of the season destroy our rest and ruin our finances.

Shopping for presents adds to the rush and stress before Christmas. We fret that we bought too little. What if someone has one more gift to open than the others? We worry if a coworker or neighbor brings us something unexpected and we have nothing to give in return.

Then the bills start to arrive. We've stretched our money beyond normal limits in the effort to satisfy every wish.

All the focus on Christmas gifts clutters our minds and steals our time with God. We concentrate on the external objects of this season more than eternal matters.

The gift of Advent doesn't cost us, but gives us priceless peace.

The gift of Advent doesn't add to our stress, but brings us joy in His birth to save us.

The gift of the coming Christ Child restores hope

and helps us look forward to His return.

Advent is the time to realize that everything we have is a gift from God.

All we hold dear comes from God: our families, our friends, our lives.

We look at our hands that write names on the gift tags and at the bottom of the cards we send, knowing He formed the muscles and nerves to make our writing possible.

We give thanks as we watch our breath made visible in the cold winter air as we sing carols at homes in the neighborhood. His Spirit moves as the music tells the good news to someone who forgot or never knew His story.

We bow our heads saying grace for the food we eat and the warmth of a safe home.

We smile with grateful hearts while keeping alive the traditions that capture the hearts of children and adults, like Advent wreaths and Sunday school pageants.

The twinkling stars in the winter sky remind us of the star that guided the wise men and we know God directs our ways.

We discover hope when we reflect on all these aspects of Advent. We experience healing as we bow down in worship of our King and Savior.

Advent surrounds us with joy and wonder as we remember all we cherish originates with God. All we hold dear comes from Him.

His gift to us—every moment.

Now the Lord of peace himself give you
peace always by all means.
The Lord be with you all.
2 Thessalonians 3:16

Consider what I say; and the Lord give
thee understanding in all things.
2 Timothy 2:7

All the Christmas presents in the world are
worth nothing without the presence of Christ.
DAVID JEREMIAH

What would it be like if you lived each day,
each breath, as a work of art in progress?
Imagine that you are a masterpiece unfolding
every second of every day, a work of
art taking form with every breath.
THOMAS CRUM

Encouragement

Plan now to keep Christ
the center of Christmas morning.
Start the day at the nativity set,
reading Luke 2 or retelling the story
of His birth in your own words.
Discuss the nonmaterial gifts you give
and receive like joy, hope, service, love.
Before opening presents, have a family prayer,
closing by singing "Happy Birthday" to Jesus.

✦

Prayer

Giver of Life, thank You for
the wonderful gifts of life, light, and love.
Let me carry within my heart the sense
of how much You love me and are
with me in every moment.

The Hospitality of an Advent Heart

O LORD God of Abraham, Isaac, and of Israel,
our fathers, keep this for ever in the imagination
of the thoughts of the heart of thy people,
and prepare their heart unto thee.
1 CHRONICLES 29:18

Our hearts need God.

In our vulnerability, we build walls around our hearts and fill them with fear, anger, and despair. We protect our hearts, fearing hurt and disappointment by others. Cruel words batter and build rough calluses around our fragile souls.

How do we open the doors of our heart to receive God in Advent? How do we create a place for the Christ Child to arrive within us?

We recognize our restlessness as we try to fill our emptiness with clutter and consumption. We know God is the answer to the peace we desire.

After we acknowledge this gnawing hunger for God, we know it is time to listen and learn from Him. The words we know so well from the story of His birth light our way.

We become like Mary and Joseph, trusting God with an uncertain future ahead.

We abandon our worries and anger as we rush to be with Him just like the shepherds hurried from their fields.

Like the angels we join in praising God and

providing goodwill for all.

Like the wise men we give gifts to help ease the way for others.

Following these models we experience release and healing as hurts and anger drain away. God's touch softens the barriers we create around our hearts and we receive the Christ Child with overwhelming thanksgiving. Once our hearts open, we reach out to help others heal.

Hospitality involves sharing our possessions, time, and selves. We break bread with our visitors and provide a warm welcoming place to stay. We give them intimate access to our rooms and even sacrifice our own comfort for their sake.

The hospitality of the heart prepares us to receive the Christ Child at Advent. With trusting vulnerability, we open our hearts to share our deepest needs with Him. We allow God to enter our most private rooms where we hide our shameful secrets. His presence will remove them, restoring light to darkness.

God doesn't ask us to be perfect; He just waits for us to be willing. We welcome Him by anticipating His coming, being ready to listen and learn, and opening the doors of our hearts with gratefulness.

Let's unwrap our hearts this Advent and make room for Christ to come in and transform us. May our hearts be a place of welcome for the newborn King.

God waits for us to draw closer to Him and soak in His wonder and the light of His coming. Come, Lord Jesus.

Create in me a clean heart,
O God; and renew a right spirit within me.
PSALM 51:10

✳

For now have I chosen and sanctified this house,
that my name may be there forever: and mine eyes
and mine heart shall be there perpetually.
2 CHRONICLES 7:16

Hospitality means primarily the creation
of free space where the stranger can enter
and become a friend instead of an enemy.
Hospitality is not to change people
but to offer them space where change
can take place. It is not to bring men
and women over to our side, but to offer
freedom not disturbed by dividing lines.

HENRI NOUWEN

We build walls around our hearts,
around our homes, around our land,
around our borders to keep out strangers,
the different, the other; to protect ourselves from
getting hurt or from having to share our space
with others. We guard our hearts, our land,
and our country with great vigilance until the
very guarding obsesses us and we become so
outwardly focused and defensive that we lose
touch with ourselves and our humanity.
In our efforts to protect and defend we
become disconnected and fragmented.

EDWINA GATELEY

Encouragement

Practice hospitality outwardly by sharing
a meal and inwardly by spending time
listening and worshiping our Savior.

✳

Prayer

Lord, break open my heart
to receive You this Christmas.
Help me see others as You see them.
Lead me to serve other as You do.
Fill me with Your love so Your love
overflows from You through me into others.
Come, Lord Jesus, come.

About the Author

Jean Wise is a writer, speaker, and retreat leader whose goal is "to know God and make Him known." She lives in northwest Ohio.